Sew Fast & Sew Easy

190 IDEAS TO SIMPLIFY YOUR SEWING

DOROTHY YODER

Carlisle Press, 2727 Twp. Rd. 421, Sugarcreek, OH 44681
© 1998 by Carlisle Press

Printed in the United States of America
Printing and design by Carlisle Printing

ISBN 1-890050-22-9

2727 TOWNSHIP RD 421
SUGARCREEK, OH 44681

CARLISLE
PRESS
WALNUT CREEK

Dedication

Dedicated to God,

the Giver of all good gifts

IV

Contents

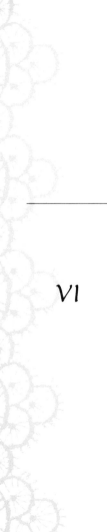

vi

Foreword

Having known Dorothy for many years, I've been witness to the fact that she's a born seamstress with an eye for detail. For a time she was employed at Chestnut Ridge Sewing where she broadened her education on sewing techniques and handy tools of the trade. She would be too modest to claim expertise, but I think she comes close.

As a mother of five, I have learned the value of being able to sew efficiently, not wasting any time. Therefore I appreciate this volume packed full of simple ways to improve my sewing speed and skills. If *Sew Fast & Sew Easy* lightens your load by saving you stitches and quickens your interest in sewing, it has accomplished the goal of the author. She delights in being a blessing to sisters in Christ as they serve Him in practical ways.

Miriam Wengerd
Keepers At Home magazine

VIII

Acknowledgments

A special thanks to Mom for her patience and support during the years I learned to sew.

To Tom and Rhoda Beachy at Chestnut Ridge Sewing for the invaluable experience I gained while working with them—thank you.

To the staff at Carlisle Press—Marvin Wengerd for your enthusiastic support, Arlen Miller and Barbara Miller for the energy and creativity that you poured into the design of this book—thank you.

Dorothy Yoder

6/16/98

x

TURK'S-CAP LILY
Lilium superbum

1

Sewing Machine

SEWING MACHINE

2

Threading

Slide a piece of white paper behind the sewing machine needle to make the eye easier to see when threading it.

When filling bobbins, pull the thread through the hole in the bobbin and hold it taut above the bobbin to get it started. Clip the thread tail closely as soon as it starts winding itself. This prevents the first few yards from tangling when filling the bobbin and enables you to use your thread down to the last inch.

Before all else fails,
read instructions!

Prevent Jamming

If the sewing machine jams when you start off, it is probably due to incorrect handling. To eliminate this problem:

1. Have the bobbin thread drawn up and laid out to the side or back.

2. The upper thread should also be laid out to the side or back. It must be held securely by threading it through the slot in the foot and then lowering the foot onto it. In cases where the foot is not designed to hold the upper thread after being lowered, hold on to the thread as you start off. If the upper thread is not held securely, it will draw down into the bobbin area as you start off, causing the machine to jam.

3. Have the thread take-up lever in its highest position when you start and stop. This is the starting and finishing point of a stitch and will aid in having threads relaxed when you remove the fabric from the machine and prevent the needle from unthreading when you restart.

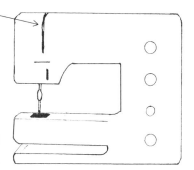

SEWING MACHINE

3

4

Use the Right Needle

Use the right size needle for the job at hand. 75/11 needles will snap when sewing denim, while 100/16 needles will make large holes and possibly punch your delicate fabric down through the needle plate.

To eliminate skipped stitches on knit fabrics, use Schmetz® stretch needles.

If your sewing machine accommodates a double needle, you will not be able to insert two needles. A double needle is simply two needles built onto a single shaft, fitting into your machine like a regular needle.

Spot Needle Size Easily

The Schmetz® needles have the size of the needle on the shank. To make them easily visible, rub the shank with chalk or soap.

SEWING MACHINE

5

Straight Rows

If you have trouble getting a straight, even stitch, try using a larger needle (the larger the number, the larger the size). A larger needle will break the fibers in the fabric to make a straight row of stitches, whereas a smaller one will jump to one side or the other. Try using the edge stitch or blind stitch foot for topstitching along the edge of collars, suspenders, etc. The width of the seam varies with different needle positions.

SEWING MACHINE

6

Make a Needle Book

Cut four 2" x 2" patches of felt or medium to heavy fabric. Run across one end with a straight stitch. Mark each "page" with a different needle size and store your sewing machine needles there between uses.

Dull Needles

Replace sewing machine needles after 8–10 hours of stitching. This will help stitch quality and prevent damage to your fabric. Save the used ones to hang posters, pictures, etc.

Use the Right Thread

SEWING MACHINE

7

Using a more expensive, good quality thread is worth your time and money. Your mending work will be reduced. We prefer the metro-sene thread; it can't be beat for quality. It does a very neat and fine job for sewing coverings. It is 100% polyester for strength and stretch, and it will not fade.

Serger cone thread is not recommended for use on the sewing machine. It is fine and smooth, made for high speed sewing. This thread is weaker than all purpose thread and should not be used in a straight-stitched seam. You will be able to purchase household cone thread, which is more expensive, but lasts a long time.

Try using a finer thread to make buttonholes on lightweight fabrics. Lingerie or darning thread both work well.

SEWING MACHINE

8

Two at a Time

If you have two sewing machines, use them both when sewing a garment that needs two different threads. That way you won't need to change spools so often.

Mark Your Seam Allowance

For a seam allowance wider than what is marked on your machine, strip a rubber band around the free arm at the proper width.

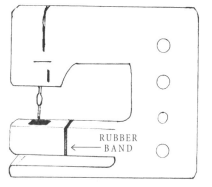

RUBBER
← BAND

Quick Measuring

For a handy measuring guide at your fingertips, tape a length of tape measure to the surface of your machine or cabinet with a piece of 2" clear packing tape.

SEWING MACHINE

9

Fill Two Bobbins

If you'll be using a lot of the same color thread in the sewing machine, fill at least two bobbins before you start. This will save the frustration of filling one halfway through a seam.

SEWING MACHINE

Adjusting Tensions

If thread tensions are out of balance, you may attempt to adjust them yourself. Follow these instructions:

1.   Remove the bobbin case and check the bobbin tension. There should be only a very light pull on the thread. There is a small screw in the flat spring that pinches the thread. To adjust, turn the screw in to tighten, or out to loosen the tension. If the spring has two screws in it, the one on the end is to fasten the spring, and the one in the middle is for adjusting.

2.   Turn the upper tension dial to a loose setting—usually a lower number.

3.   On a firm fabric, sew a short row of wide zigzags. There will be loops on the bottom of the fabric.

Adjusting Tensions *(continued)*

4. Turn the upper tension dial to a slightly tighter setting. Sew another row of zigzags. The loops on the bottom of the fabric should be smaller.

5. Repeat step 4 until the loops on the bottom of the fabric shrink to small dots at the outer edge of the zigzags. The tensions will now be balanced.

SEWING MACHINE

11

Teach Your Children

When teaching young children to sew, set the machine at a shortened 3-step zigzag stitch. The foot pedal can be pushed down all the way but will not feed as fast as a straight stitch would. This allows the child time to learn to guide the fabric as it feeds through.

SEWING MACHINE

12

Cleaning Your Machine

A turkey baster or an empty dishwashing soap bottle is a great way to blast the fuzzies out of your sewing machine or serger. It's cheaper than "canned" air!

Use a Q-tip to clean your sewing machine. It gets into places a brush can't reach, and cleans up excess oil as well.

Installing a Zipper

The Bernina buttonhole foot (#3) makes sewing a hidden zipper go quickly and easily. Unzip zipper and press coils open with a warm iron. Guide the flattened coil into a groove. You might have to adjust your needle position slightly.

Hemming
with a Hemmer Foot

To make starting easy when hemming with a narrow hemmer foot, clip a small diagonal off the corner. Make several stitches on the edge (within $^1/_8$") of the side to be hemmed. Raise the foot without clipping the threads and pull the fabric through, along with about 3" of thread. Bring the fabric around to the front and, using the thread tails as an aid, feed the fabric into the scroll of the foot. Lower the foot and sew, guiding the fabric carefully. This foot can be used to hem ruffles, dresses, sheets, shirts, etc.

13

SEWING MACHINE

14

Machine Repair

Be sure to know the model number of your sewing machine before asking your dealer for parts.

Always include your bobbin case and foot control when your machine needs to be taken in for adjustments or repairs. The trouble may not always be in the machine itself.

When we see the lilies

    Spinning in distress,

Taking thought to

    Manufacture loveliness;

When we see the birds all

    Building barns for store,

'Twill be time for us to worry—

    Not before!

                —Selected

SEWING MACHINE

15

Notes

SEWING MACHINE

16

The greatest invention since
the sewing machine is
the seam ripper.

Laundry & Pressing

LILY OF THE VALLEY
Convallaria majalis

17

18

Preshrink Fabric

To avoid shrinking clothing, preshrink fabric in hot water and detergent before cutting garment. Detergent softens fabric for maximum shrinkage.

Remove Candle Wax

If you have candle wax on clothing, place a paper towel on it. Iron over it with a hot iron. The wax melts and is absorbed into the paper towel.

Remove Stains

Wisk is great for soaking soiled cuffs and collars. Amway Prewash also works well.

Ink Stains

Hair spray works well as a prewash for ballpoint ink marks. Spray, then launder as usual.

Don't Set Stains

Hot water tends to set some stains in clothes. Presoak the laundry in cold water, then wash in warm water. What doesn't dissolve in the presoak will wash out.

Remove or Improve Creases

Use white vinegar to renew trouser leg creases and take out old dress hem marks. It can also be used when making a new garment and you want something to lie flat. Put vinegar in a spray bottle to use. Do not use apple cider vinegar—it makes brown stains.

Pressing is Essential

Press your work as you go. It makes it a lot easier to get a proper fit. If you're short on time while sewing, take time to press all seams when you're done.

Flat Seams

A seam that doesn't lie flat after it has been pressed can be brought to submission with a clapper, a smooth piece of wood. Or, an unheated iron can be placed on top of the seam immediately after pressing. Hold in place for 30 seconds or until cooled.

Keep Iron Clean

Use an appliqué pressing sheet with fusible interfacings. It has a plastic texture and will protect your iron and ironing board cover from sticky residue. The sticky substance on the sheet peels off, making it reusable.

Iron Cleaner

Hot iron cleaner (Iron-Off™ by Dritz) is a great, safe way to clean your iron without scratching its surface. Follow instructions on the package. Never use a chore ball or SOS pad. They will scratch the soleplate, where particles set in, making it worse than before.

A brand new iron might need to be cleaned before it's used. The soleplate often has a film on it which will transfer to the garment that is being ironed. Take good care of it from the start and the soleplate will serve you well for years.

Mark Size on Clothes

Sorting and folding laundry on washdays is made easier for everyone if the size of the pattern (which is usually about the child's age) is marked on the inside back with a permanent marker. That way a small child knows which is his and also which is front and back.

Mark Your Mending

When you're folding laundry and notice a spot that needs mending, mark it with a safety pin. Later, when you get to the mending, you won't need to spend extra time looking over the garment trying to decide if it was a popped seam, a missing button, or a hem that needed adjusting.

Sew Much Love

—Mrs. David Vendley

That needle poking to and fro
Means so much more than you may know.
Each snap, each button, each shirt, each dress,
Contains something you'll never guess.
Each garment Mom makes, from the start,
Contains a small piece of her heart.
With every snip she adds her love,
And whispers a prayer to God above.

"Dear Father, bless the one who wears this,
Protect and guide them with Your kindness.
Give them strength from day to day,
That from all sin they'll turn away."

Then into each and every seam
She presses in her fondest dream
That each one in her family
Will join her in eternity.

So next time Mom makes you any clothes,
Know that, in it, her love shows.
It's more than just a thing to wear,
It's a symbol of Mom's loving care.

Patterns & Cutting

DELPHINIUM
Delphinium sp.

25

26

Which Side is Right?

If you have a fabric with which it is hard to tell the right side from the wrong, be sure to cut all your pattern pieces with the fabric folded the same way, and be careful to stack the pieces with the same sides together. When you start sewing, you'll have less guesswork and eyestrain!

When Two Pieces Look Alike

When cutting a garment that has very similar fronts and backs, make an extra large notch point in the center of the back piece. You will immediately be able to differentiate front and back, and the notch point can easily be trimmed off once the seams are sewn.

Tried & True Patterns

A good pattern is a must. Get tried and true patterns unless you're an advanced sewer and like to change some details here and there. Plainly marked patterns help greatly—i.e. how much seam allowance, etc.

Organizing Patterns

Manila folders taped at both sides make excellent pattern keepers. Write the contents on the tab and you'll be able to find them at a glance.

Strengthen Patterns

To keep an original pattern from getting dog-eared and tattered, apply a lightweight, fusible, non-woven interfacing.

Keep Scissors Handy

To keep a small pair of scissors handy when you sew, tie them around your neck with a 3- to 4-foot ribbon or string.

Tracing Patterns

Use a dry soap scrap to trace around patterns onto fabric. Unopened Campbell's soup cans (or any brand) work well to hold the patterns in place.

Quick Cutting

A rotary cutter is a marvelous time saver in cutting garments, quilts, coverings, you name it! It allows you to cut several thicknesses at one time. It is well worth the investment!

When purchasing a rotary cutting mat, be sure to buy Olfa or Omnigard. These brands are self-healing, unlike the white ones, which tend to "catch" the fabric in the grooves made by the cutter.

When using a pinking rotary cutter, don't use it along a straight edge (ruler, etc.). This tends to dull the blade faster.

Adjusting Patterns

If you don't want to chop off a larger size pattern for a smaller one, make a 1" cut with a razor blade or rotary cutter every 2", then trace with a marker.

For non-stretch dresses, add $5/8$" to 1" on fold to the center back when cutting. Stitch several inches on the pattern line at top and $1^1/_2$" at bottom, leaving the center open. This provides extra give without adding to the neck and waist.

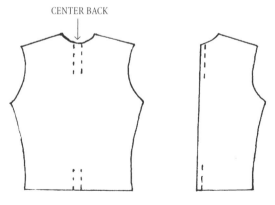

CENTER BACK

Adjusting Patterns *(continued)*

To alter the width of a shoulder, cut into the pattern, adjust, and resume cutting. This method will retain the shape of the armhole.

PATTERN WILL LOOK LIKE THIS

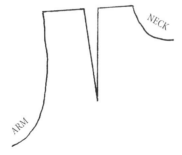

If you make any changes in your pattern while cutting or sewing, be sure to mark it on the pattern guidesheet or the pattern itself. If you don't, you may be surprised at how well you forget!

Fitting a Rounded Back

To fit someone with a rounded back, cut in the pattern from back to mid arm and pull the pattern apart. The rounder the back, the farther the pattern should be pulled apart. The dress will fit nicely over the rounded back.

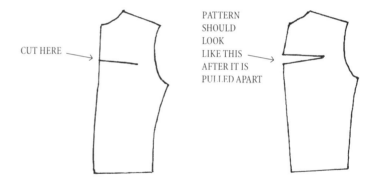

CUT HERE →

PATTERN
SHOULD
LOOK
LIKE THIS →
AFTER IT IS
PULLED APART

NOTE: Your pattern back must be in two pieces to do this.

Correcting Cape Fit

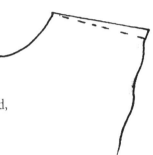

A cape that is wavy as it hangs from
the shoulder needs to be tapered
more at the shoulder seam. A seam
that is tapered too much will look stretched,
puckering towards the neck.

Stitch the shoulder seam the width of the seam allowance up to the hem-
line. At this point, pivot and taper off about $1/8$". Press seam open and the
hem will not be strained across the shoulder, as it is folded.

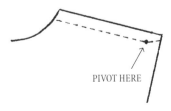

PIVOT HERE

34

Little Girls' Dress Patterns

For the skirts of little girls' dresses, measure waist to ankle bone; this is your length. Measure waist x 2 for width.

Any store dress or blouse pattern will do for the top. Gather the top of the skirt to fit.

If the pattern has puffy sleeves you don't like, trim the "arch" to be a duller angle.

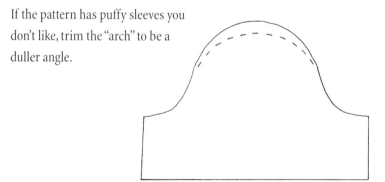

Minimize Pattern Pieces

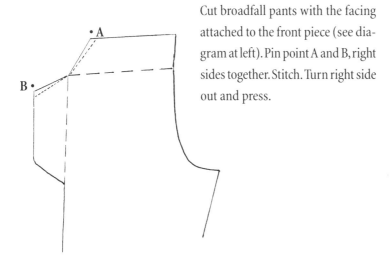

Cut broadfall pants with the facing attached to the front piece (see diagram at left). Pin point A and B, right sides together. Stitch. Turn right side out and press.

When sewing together leg seams, just catch all layers and reinforce at pockets.

Pattern Weights

If you'd like pattern weights but don't wish to spend much for them, check a hardware shop or even around a repair shop. Often you may find large nuts or similar parts that, with good cleaning and a coat of paint to keep them from rusting, will work wonderfully to hold your patterns firmly.

The trouble with
        making mental notes
    is that
    the ink fades so fast.

Paul Sweeney

*E*lastic

EUROPEAN PRIMROSE
Primula auricula

37

ELASTIC

Preshrink Elastic

Rather than suffer the shrinkage of elastic after the garment is made, prewash the elastic before it's applied.

Measuring Elastic

To measure elastic for sleeves, panties, etc., measure with a measuring tape if possible, then add one inch. This inch allows for the seam and for shrinkage. You should have less trouble with its becoming too tight or too loose when using this rule of thumb.

Make an Elastic Dispenser

If you buy elastic in bulk and need a convenient way to store it, an empty Baby Wipes™ container will do the job perfectly! Thread the elastic through the hole in the top (which might have to be slightly enlarged).

ELASTIC

39

Use a Zigzag Stitch

Use a zigzag stitch to sew elastic. It is a stretch stitch and will not easily break the thread.

ELASTIC

40

Non-Irritating Bands

Sew on elastic for underwear with wrong side of elastic to wrong side of fabric. Turn elastic up and put the sewn edge down over the seam and sew again with a small zigzag seam. (Elastic will be standing up with right side out.) Trim off any excess fabric that pokes out, working very carefully so as not to cut elastic. This method keeps the edge of the elastic from irritating the skin.

When sewing elastic on the legs of panties, do not stretch it when sewing it onto the crotch. It gives a more comfortable fit and does not tend to "dig in" while you are wearing the garment.

Working with Casing

When making a garment with a waistline casing, use a small strip of fusible interfacing to hold down the seam allowances. The elastic will slide in without catching in the seams.

ELASTIC

41

Smooth the Way

Rounding the end of the elastic before inserting it into the casing eliminates the frustration of the end catching on the seam allowances.

ELASTIC

Prevent Elastic Rolling

To keep elastic from rolling, in waistbands especially, stitch in the ditch of the side seams on top of the elastic.

42

LIVE-FOREVER
Sedum telephioides

43

Interfacing

INTERFACING

44

Right Side Up

The "sticky" or fusible side of interfacings will either be shiny or have small raised dots. Be sure to have this side turned down when ironing.

Fusible or Stitchable?

Use fusible interfacings whenever possible. Since some interfacings will be slightly firmer after application, you may want to use a stitchable for a softer, more subtle shape. Stitchables will become softer after laundering.

Store on Tubes

Interfacings can be stored neatly on cardboard tubes left over from Christmas wrappings. Secure with rubber bands. Instructions can be tucked inside the tube and held in place with a paper clip.

INTERFACING

45

Handy Pockets

Use the printed plastic interfacing instructions to make a pocket for each type of interfacing. Fold it in half and sew the sides together. Store the interfacing and scraps in the pocket and you'll always have the instructions handy!

INTERFACING

46

Prewash to Prevent Shrinkage

If the interfacing wants to bubble on the ready-made garment after laundering, it's a sign of shrinkage. For best results, prewash the fabric and the interfacing before cutting.

When prewashing interfacing, place in a basin of hot water and let soak for 20 minutes. It will not damage the fusing agent, which is not activated until it reaches 300° or more. Do not agitate or you might dislodge the fusing resin. Hang it on a towel on the rack to dry. Do not bunch up or twist.

Buttonhole Stabilizers

Cut 2" x 12" strips of iron-on interfacing and keep them handy to stabilize buttons and buttonholes. Iron on **inside** of **facing**.

INTERFACING

47

Or, use freezer paper as a stabilizer under buttonholes. With shiny side to fabric, press paper with a moderately hot iron. The paper will stick to the fabric and hold it in place until the buttonholes are made. The paper is then easily peeled away. A word of caution: freezer paper does to needles what paper does to scissors.

INTERFACING

48

Trimming Seams

When using sew-in interfacing in seams, especially collars, cuffs, etc., trim interfacing down to seam, trim next fabric layer to half of seam width, and leave the other layer as is. This eliminates bulky seams.

Cover Entire Piece

Never fuse interfacing directly on the outside garment unless it will cover the entire pattern piece (collars, for example). The fusing line will be visible from the outside, and might cause only fused area to shrink.

Little Girl's
Apron Lining Technique

INTERFACING

49

1. Make lining smaller by trimming $1/8$" from neck, armholes, and front. (This keeps lining from showing when apron is finished.)

2. Sew shoulder seams in both lining and outside fabric.

3. Match lining to outside fabric right sides together at neck, armholes, and front. Stitch using small stitches at curves and corners.

4. Trim and press the seams you have just sewn. Also clip and notch where necessary. Trim curved seams with pinking shears.

(continued)

Little Girl's
Apron Lining Technique

(continued)

5. Turn apron to right side by reaching through front shoulders and pulling back through.

6. Press thoroughly. Sew side seams by matching underarm seams. Sew lining front and back right sides together and apron fabric front and back right sides together at side seams. Press side seams open.

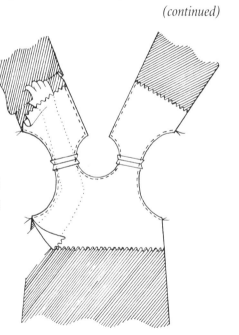

PETUNIA
Petunia sp.

51

Coverings

Measuring for Size

I've had good success with the following method, but have used it only on little girls.

1. Measure the distance from the bottom tip of one ear to the bottom tip of the other.

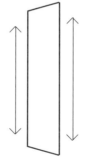

2. Add 1" to this measurement for the front of the band.

3. Add another inch for the back of the band ($^{1}/_{2}$" on each side).

Measuring for Size *(continued)*

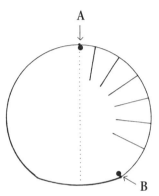

4. Divide measurement #3 by two and subtract $1/4$". This measurement will be for the crown from center (A) to tip (B) after the pleats are pinned in.

Purchasing Covering Material

Always buy covering material by the even foot or yard (2, 4, 6, etc.). An average "feddahdale" (band) is 20" long. One yard of fabric is enough for $1^1/2$ "feddahdala." Also, you can count on one average size covering per foot.

Lining the Covering

If you need a fusible interfacing to line the covering, do the fusing before you cut the covering at all. Interfacing has a way of shifting and shrinking and that will not be noticeable on the covering after it's made, if it's cut after fusing.

When fusing nylon netting and Shirtailor interfacing together, iron the interfacing side first with a moderately hot iron. This activates the "fingers" of the interfacing which reach out through the nylon. The other side then needs to be smoothed down with a warm iron. The iron will get sticky, but can easily be cleaned with Iron-Off (see page 22).

Keep iron moving slowly at all times when ironing interfacings. If the iron rests on one spot for any length of time, the iron mark will remain. For the first initial bonding, move iron lightly and gently over interfacing so as not to stretch or shift it.

Ironing Surface

After nylon covering is cut, move to a hard surface for ironing. A Formica topped surface is fine. With a moderately hot iron, move quickly over nylon side, pressing down as you go. An ironing board will not work, as it is too soft and porous. Use this same type of surface for pleats.

Check Fuse

Check if the fusing job has been properly done by folding the covering in half, right sides together. Make a crease at the center. Open it up, and you should be able to see if the netting stands away from the interfacing at the center fold.

Mark the Pattern

If you don't have the pleats marked on the pattern and you do each covering individually, mark the pattern as you would a covering. Then each time you make a covering, you will be able to make the markings with a seam ripper or yarn darner needle, and you're ready to make the pleats.

Use a Marker

Mark the pleats with a disappearing ink marker. The purple dot shows up while you're working on the pleat, whereas the hole made by the needle fades into the fabric again. The dots will disappear within eight hours.

Protective Coating

Spray coverings with an even coat of plastic spray or clear paint before making pleats. The pleats will hold their place much better, and the crimping will have a crisper and more defined appearance as well.

As for plastic spray and clear paint, I prefer using clear paint because it dries faster, and it takes less to stiffen the covering. However, I think it does tend to yellow faster. Cheaper brands definitely turn yellow.

COVERINGS

57

Mark Pleats
Before Crimping

Mark all the pleats with a crease before crimping. Fold covering in half and with a stitch length of 4–5, stitch around the outside of the area to be crimped (at the end of each pleat). For nylon coverings, fold and turn inside out.

Press pleats in nylon coverings with a moderately hot iron. If the nylon starts to shrivel or bubble, it is too hot. The pleats are much easier to control if the crease is ironed in rather than finger pressed.

Crimping

The very first row in crimping needs to be very narrow—half the width of the rest of the crimps. Since it is done on the fold, it will double in width when opened up.

COVERINGS

59

To make crimping easier, use a small spatula to hold the crease of the previous row as you push against it with a dull paring knife, forming the next row. This method produces an even crimping all the way across. (The first two rows need to be done by hand.)

Shaping the Crown

When the pleating is done, take a small bowl or platter, about the size of the crimped area, and lay it on the inside of the covering, edges even with the bottom side pleats or the bottom pleats, if any. Push down on the bowl to keep it from sliding and with your free hand fold the covering up around the edge of the bowl (around the bottom only). This will form a nice, round crown. This process is necessary only on coverings that are crimped all the way down.

Making the Pleats

Pin and finger press the pleats in the bottom first. You will only need to guess how wide the pleats should be. Fitting comes later. If you take this step, finishing the covering is a breeze after the two parts are joined. Remove pins and proceed with top pleats.

Pleats need to be pinned in to keep their proper shape and position. Where the pleat folds, often times either the main covering part juts our further, or the pleat itself does. This will not hurt the covering as long as the pleat is lying naturally flat. There should be no "dip" below the pleat when pressed together between thumb and finger.

COVERINGS

61

Making the Pleats *(continued)*

Pin in the pleat before you finger press it. Take only a small "bite" with the pin; a large bite will widen the pleat in the center. Work on the inside, with the crown of the covering propped up straight from the dot. Always make the point of the pleat first. Work your way back toward the pin, pushing the excess fabric away from the fold.

If you're not sure how wide to make the pleats, make them scant rather than too wide. A narrow pleat that has been pressed in can easily be widened without affecting the "curve" of the pleat.

For a more consistent sizing from one covering to the next, measure each side along the edge, from the center to the tip; sides should be same. Adjust the width of the pleats as needed.

Hemming the Forepiece

The "feddahdale" (front band) needs to be hemmed. It can be folded in once or twice. It's all personal preference—there's no right or wrong way. Nylon coverings I do fold in twice because the nylon tends to catch in the hair. Press it with a warm iron as you fold it.

Hem the band as closely to the inside fold as possible. The closer the stitching, the more uniform the shaping along the front edge of the covering. Stitch with a length of $2^{1}/_{2}$ to 3.

COVERINGS

64

Fight Sag

When a covering seems to sag in the back, the top pleats need to be wider. If the pattern tends to do that, make the pleats at the top wider and taper the width along down the side. The pleats don't all *have* to be the same size, as long as they're uniform. Likewise, when a covering seems to stand out too straight from the top, the top pleats are too wide.

Securing the Pleats

Sew around the outside edge of the pleats to secure them. For organdy coverings with the band sewn on by machine, this is not necessary. For nylon coverings, ironing is so much easier without the pins.

Ironing Pleats

After the pleats are sewn in on nylon coverings, they need to be ironed from the inside. Spray lightly with most any brand of spray starch (*not plastic spray*). Press with a moderately hot iron. Immediately after removing the iron, press the pleat firmly with your finger. You will probably need to spray after ironing every two pleats. *Do not iron the bottom pleats until the covering is all done.* If this step is done well, you will never need to iron the pleats again.

If pleats do need to be ironed after the covering is finished, spray with starch and use the tip of the iron to press from the inside. Smooth the pleat down with your finger immediately after removing iron. Be careful not to iron wrinkles into the front band.

COVERINGS

65

Pin Forepiece to Main Piece

Be sure to pin the front band onto the main part. Place a pin in the center then work down each side, being careful not to distort the band. Pin between every pleat, again taking only a small "bite" with the pin. Be sure to pin down the ends as well.

66

A Smooth Seam

After the band is pinned on, you will be able to see the shape the covering will be. Look between the band and the main part where the pins join the two. You might see all sorts of bubbles, bumps, and horns. *You will not need to change the pleats.* The shape is now totally controlled by the way the band is pinned on. To get rid of a bubble, slide the band *away* every so slightly from the edge of the crown. If an area seems too flat, move the band *toward* the edge. If you *are* already at the edge, you'll have to work with the bubbles on each side of it.

Rounding the Covering

If the covering seems rather square, slide the *ends* of the band approximately $1/4$" away from the edge of the crown. Don't remove the pin just above the bottom side pleat. If there seems to be any strain on the band, you've gone too far. Then you'll probably have to work with a bubble at the bottom side pleat.

Stitch Twice

When the covering is shaped properly, stitch inside along the edge of the band. If you can't see through the fabric, you'll just have to guess a little. After the first stitching, trim what extends past the band. The second row of stitching might be exactly the same as the first, but it makes a stronger seam and adds more body to the covering.

Turning it Right

Turning the band right side out can be surprisingly easy. With the band of the lower right hand side in your left hand, pull gently on each pleat with your right hand until completely straightened, turning the band as you go. By the halfway point, it will practically straighten itself.

Guiding Seam Allowances

Press machine-stitched seams toward band with your finger. At each end of the band where it joins the crown, slide the band back to have it overlap the seam approximately $1/8$", more or less as suitable. Work the fullness into the seam, moving toward the center. If the covering ended up with bubbles, slide the band back slightly and finger press. At this point you can still somewhat shape the covering.

Topstitching

Nylon covering seams do not need to be topstitched from the outside. In fact, as you stitch around from the inside, it's amazing how the crown shapes up. It is very important to keep the covering in its naturally round state as you sew. Don't scrunch it down so you can "see" where you're going.

To stitch around the inside, Bernina owners use foot #0 or #1 and move needle position one right of center. You will not be able to see through the covering very well, so guide the center line of the foot along the outer row of stitches. Non-Bernina owners will need to find what works best for them.

COVERINGS

69

Try It On!

Once the bottom pleats are pinned in, the covering needs to be tried on for size. Save yourself some discomfort by pushing the pins in all the way before fitting. If the covering seems too tight and small, loosen the pleats a bit. If it's too large, widen the pleats. Many different sizes can be made from one pattern because of this flexibility.

Shape the Neckline

Trim around the bottom, especially the band, to round the neckline. At the seams, leave the band just a mite longer than the crown. When you're stitching around the inside, you won't need to pivot at the center. Instead, you can round the corner, making a neat finish.

Facing

Do not try to sew in the bottom pleats before you attach the facing. The covering will not have the same fit after it's done. The truest fit I've found is not from using a bias strip of organdy or bias tape, but a fairly tightly woven organdy cut as a facing, with the same curve as the covering. Place the covering on the fabric and with a pencil or (my sewing buddy) a disappearing ink marker, trace the neckline. Cut a strip $1^1/_2$–2" wide and pin it onto the covering. If the facing doesn't fit quite right, slide the excess facing over the edge. Place a pin in the center, at the seams and at each end. Sew around the inside, backstitching at each end.

COVERINGS

71

Trimming the Facing

Before turning the facing under, clip the facing all the way to the seam, between the seam and the bottom pleats. Fold it under, pin, and topstitch around the inside. Trim facing fairly close to the seam.

The Wonder Iron

A good ironing job does *wonders* for a covering!

Iron organdy coverings with a folded white handkerchief, and your hand as the "ironing board." Press the seam first. Start at the center, working down each side. Iron the point of the pleat first and work back toward the band.

The Bow

Making a "shlup" (bow) from fabric has just become fun and easy! Cut a length of organdy (eg. 3" x 6"). Fold in half lengthwise, wrong sides together, and sew a $1/4$" seam (or more to suite your taste) along the fold. Press the seam open, cut off the width you need, and fold under the raw edge. No more fussing with little pieces!

COVERINGS

73

Black Coverings

Black Nu-Life color spray works very well to make nylon coverings black. The smell does not linger on the covering as that of paint. It can be sprayed on either before or after the covering is made.

COVERINGS

Notes

Bits & Pieces

MARSH MARIGOLD
Caltha palustris

75

Zigzag or Serge

Zigzag the edges of cut pieces of fabric if it isn't knit, unless you're fortunate enough to own a serger.

Choosing Thread Color

If you cannot exactly match thread color to your medium to dark fabric, use a darker shade. It will blend in better than a lighter shade. For lighter colored fabrics, choose a lighter shade.

Hemming

When hemming knits, use a zigzag rather than a straight stitch, as it will have more give and prevent puckering.

Needle Preening

Make a small bag out of tightly woven fabric and pack it with fine sand. When your sewing needle feels dull or develops a burr that catches on fine fabric, poke it into the sand a few times to sharpen it. An ornamental sandbag would make a nice gift or craft item for sale, perhaps with an attached card bearing instructions such as "Jab your needles into me and they'll stay as sharp as they can be!" Don't store your needles in the sandbag, or they'll likely become rusty.

Tough Thread

For longer wear, stitch gloves, slippers, and booties with dental floss instead of thread. To keep the strands from fraying while you sew, rub a piece of beeswax over the floss every few stitches.

Mark It

A disappearing ink marker is a must in every sewing room. Use it to mark the length of buttonholes, button placement, darts, covering pleats, etc. It's also ideal for quilters who can no longer see the original lines well. Mark it as you go. It disappears in 8–12 hours.

Buttons and Buttonholes

Secure your buttons temporarily with Scotch tape to keep them from sliding around under the presser foot, while sewing them on.

Keep a needle threaded with 4–6 threads to do spur-of-the-moment mending on pants buttons.

To thread a needle for hand sewing snaps, buttons, etc., insert the "fold" of a length of thread into the eye of the needle, pull it even with the open ends, and tie a knot. You now have 4 threads working for you!

Don't risk a ripped buttonhole! Place a pin at each end to keep the seam ripper from slicing through the bar tack, or fold the buttonhole in half lengthwise and cut with scissors.

Buttons and Buttonholes

(continued)

BITS & PIECES

80

A bar tack on a buttonhole does not need to be stitched more than 5 times. A pileup of thread keeps the fabric from feeding smoothly under the presser foot.

To find the size needed for a buttonhole, place the button on the fabric and make a dot on each side. A vanishing ink marker is great for this.

To sew on buttons, drop feed dogs* and set a zigzag wide enough to stitch across to each hole. Turn the hand wheel to test clearance.

*Feed dogs are the teeth under the foot that feed the material through as you sew.

Buttons and Buttonholes

(continued)

Removing the staple *before* you pluck the button from the card is much easier than trying to pry it from a single button.

Use 6-strand embroider floss to sew on buttons by hand. One pass through the shank and you're done!

When you finish a garment, sew an extra button in an inconspicuous place, so you have a match later when you need a replacement.

To prevent those buttonholes from looking fuzzy and frayed, make a duplicate buttonhole on top of the original after it's cut open.

Pucker Yoke
on Little Girl's Dress

For a little girl's knit dress, let the yoke pucker a bit when you're pinning it onto the gathered skirt. This will eliminate a "stretched" look.

An Ounce of Prevention

When making dresses, stitch the waist seam and the sleeve seams twice. You will have less mending.

Lengthening a Cotton Dress

Would you like to let the hem down on that cotton dress, but the crease would show? Sew $1/2$"–1" (or whatever width you prefer) around the bottom of the hem, in a matching thread. Let down your hem. You will have a becoming tuck as well as a lengthened dress!

BITS & PIECES

83

Use Leftover Thread

Use up odd-colored leftover spools of thread when piecing comforts or quilts.

Pleating Skirts

When laying pleats in your skirt, pin, then sew over it with a stitch length of 3–4; gather just a little. They will lie down much nicer than if they're just laid in.

Sewing Slips

Save time on wash day and sewing day by taking undershirts or T-strap shirts and sewing on a skirt using tee shirt knit. Be sure to make the skirt wide enough. If they are too tight, they tend to ride up and defeat the purpose. Stretch the shirt as you sew it onto the skirt, and it will automatically gather in a neat way. Use a zigzag stitch, sew twice, and presto! Only one piece of clothing instead of two on wash day!

Recycle Sleepers

Renew those sleepers with cracked, worn-out plastic feet. Cut the bottoms of the feet off just above the plastic. Take a larger stocking with worn-out feet and cut off the feet. Fold the rest of the stocking in half and cut. Sew one end shut on each half and sew open end to cut-off sleeper foot (like ribbing). Foot of sleeper will fit on child like a tube sock.

BITS & PIECES

85

Pin, Pin, Pin!

I have been sewing for years and still do a lot of pinning before making actual seams. However, not everyone may find this necessary.

Taking Out Stitches

Instead of picking at all the stitches with a seam ripper when you need to open a seam, make short work of it by pulling the thread tail back over the stitches with a quick jerk. Each snap of the thread leaves another tail on the other side.

Left over Right, or Vice Versa?

Men's/Boys' shirts and coats, etc. close left over right. Women's clothes close right over left. An easy way to remember: boys are leftovers!

Topstitching a White Cape

The blind stitch or edge stitch foot makes topstitching a white cape fun and easy. Sew directly on the bias tape with the needle positioned to the left of the guide.

Remove Selvage

Always cut the selvage off of fabric. This is the edge that was fastened to the loom. These threads are weak and will continue to shrink with wash and wear.

Clip Rounded Seams

Clip rounded seams—collars, sleeves, etc.—for a neater, flatter finish. For inside curves, cut notches. For tight curves, clip every $^1/_2$".

Reinforce Seams

Sew seams twice or even three times, especially those hard-to-get-later seams (a lined coat, for example). Be sure everything is correct and fits before doing so! It really saves on mending open seams later on.

Patching

When patching pants, do a good job of pinning on your patch. It helps keep it straight and easy to work with.

BITS & PIECES

89

When patching pants with side seams, use a patch large enough to be sewn into the seams on both sides.

Thread Organizing

For those of you without a spool rack, have someone make dividers for your drawer to store your thread horizontally. If one layer isn't enough, make a tray to fit on top. A drawer holds more thread that way, plus you'll be able to find the color you're looking for without holding up each spool!

Backstitch to Secure Thread

To secure the last stitch when hand stitching, make an extra backstitch before tying the knot.

Neck Openings on Dresses

Don't cut the slit in the cape or dress front until after it's stitched. Press a crease on the fold of the fabric and/or mark the center line with a pencil or marker (preferably disappearing ink) the length of the opening.

Iron a strip of interfacing onto the **facing** of the front of the cape or dress. For fabrics that fray easily, this will help in the prevention of fraying. For stretchy fabrics, it will keep it from stretching, thus eliminating buckling. Have the interfacing turned up when sewing.

(continued)

Neck Openings on Dresses

(continued)

To stitch around the "opening," use a short, narrow zigzag. You have a much stronger seam and less chance of fraying. Set the stitch length at $1^1/2$ and the stitch width at 1. As you come to the end of the first side, stop with your needle down on the right of the zigzag. Pivot. Make a complete zigzag and stop with needle down. Pivot again and resume stitching. Now, cut slit between stitching.

Gathering

For fast and easy gathering, stitch two rows $^1/_8$" apart and pull both threads simultaneously, until desired fullness. Sew between the two rows of stitching when attaching to another piece. Remove thread that shows.

For a fine, even gather, sew at a stitch length of 3 or less. The smaller the stitch, the finer the gather. Try a sample stitching on your fabric to test the stitch length. Finer fabrics will need a shorter stitch length.

BITS & PIECES

93

Belts

Are you one of those who would like to have belt clips on your belt or apron, but your waistline varies too much? Take heart! Using a saftey pin, you will be able to make a movable "eye."

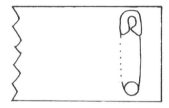

Place the safety pin inside your belt with the shaft of the pin showing on the outside, approximately the length of the clip.

When you're sewing the belt clip or hook onto the belt, make sure you stitch onto the stiffening, being careful not to catch the outside fabric. This makes a much stronger hold and eliminates stretched fabric.

Fraying

For edges that fray easily—for example, ribbon used for covering strings—melt the ends only slightly with a match or lighter.

Slip Straps

$^5/_8$" Grosgrain ribbon is wonderful for straps on homemade slips. They cannot be adjusted after they're stitched, which means they won't self-adjust, either!

Turn It Right Side Out

Tie a string onto the end of a large safety pin. When suspenders, tie backs, etc. need to be turned right side out, drop the safety pin down the tube, fasten it to the other end, and pull it back through with the string.

Appliquéing Tip

Use Wonder Under or Heat-N-Bond on projects such as quiet books, burp diapers, etc. that require appliquéing. Ask for more instructions at your local fabric/sewing store.

Keep Your Thimble in Place

Blow into your thimble before placing it on your finger. The moisture from your breath will keep it from sliding around.

Placing Snaps

To determine where the second part of the snap belongs, sew the protruding side on first, then rub the tip with a piece of white chalk. Press it onto the opposite side of the garment, and the white dot will tell you just where the other half belongs.

BITS & PIECES

98

Seam Roll

Try using a length of a 1" dowel rod as a seam roll to press the seams of suspenders or apron strings. You will be able to press the seam without making an inside-out press mark on each side.

Pressed for Time

When you need to press seams while you're sewing, why not try to do a shirt or two from your ironing basket while the iron's hot?

Recycle Towels

Recycle your old, frayed bath towels by cutting them into washrag-size pieces and finishing off the edges with a serger. They make great rags.

BITS & PIECES

99

Pantyhose Patching

When only one leg of your pantyhose develops a runner, cut off the good one at the crotch curve, and when you have another good leg, serge or sew the two together and you have a "new" pair.

BITS & PIECES

100

Mark It for Future Reference

When you make a child's garment with a pattern you like, on a $2^1/_2$" length of bias tape, write the size, pattern number, and brand name with a permanent marker such as Identi-Pen. Stitch it inside the back of the garment, and you'll have all this information for later use!

Backstitch in Place

Instead of backstitching at the end of a seam, turn the stitch length and width to 0 and make a few stitches. This will secure the stitches without the bulk of backstitching.

What Can I Do, Mom?

Entertain a preschooler in the sewing room with a darning or tapestry needle threaded with yarn or heavy thread and a supply of buttons. They can spend hours making a necklace. Older children can sew them on an old shirt or dress, or on scrap fabric.

BITS & PIECES

101

Pins Prevent Clogging

To avoid those clogged, hardened tips on seam sealant (Fray-Check, etc.) or glue, simply leave a large pearl-tipped pin in the opening. The pin will easily slide out, leaving a clear opening.

Use the Right Pins

Long, fine pins with large heads are easier to handle and gentler on hands when you're working with firm fabrics.

102

Organize Sewing Notions

Store your carded buttons, snaps, needles, etc. in a ring binder. The cards can be flipped around until you have the one you're looking for, then simply open the ring and remove it. A wire hanger can also be used for this purpose.

To keep your thread compartment neat and orderly, mark the slit on the spool end with a marker. You will then easily be able to find it, insert the thread, and snip off the excess.

Time Savers

Force your machine to go fast and train yourself to keep up. It makes a big difference in straight side seams, for example, whether you sew at a normal pace or as fast as you can.

A magnetic pin catcher is a necessity in your sewing room. It keeps your pins neatly within reach. If the pins fall on the floor, hold the catcher over them and they will jump up to it! Even children enjoy picking up pins this way.

Time Savers *(continued)*

Always make a garment in the same sequence. It's amazing how much time you save just in knowing which step is next.

Continuous sewing is another way of speeding up the sewing process. Sew as many pieces as possible without clipping the thread from the machine. When you're on piece #4, pieces #1 and #2 can be clipped and joined to make piece #5.

Stop Runs in Hose

A seam sealant like Fray-Check™ or No-Fray™ will stop runs in pantyhose.

Make It Come Out Even

When two pieces of fabric are being sewn together (skirts, pants, etc.) and one piece is slightly longer than the other, make sure the longer piece is on the bottom. The top piece can be "stretched" somewhat to make up for the fullness in the bottom piece.

106

Don't Lose Those Mittens

Sew buttons onto the cuffs of your child's mittens. When the child removes his/her wraps, the mittens can easily be buttoned into the coat button-holes.

Counted Cross Stitch Made Easy

Use a fine point washable ink marker to outline each color of the complete pattern on the cross stitch fabric. No more endless counting! The marker lines wash out easily after the project is done.

Facing for a Side Opening

Instead of cutting two separate pieces for the facing of the side opening in a dress, cut only one 4" x 8" strip. With right sides together, sew strip onto dress front and back. Turn seam allowance toward facing and topstitch. Pin dress, right sides together, matching waistline seams. Sew side seam. No more embarrassing gaps!

BITS & PIECES

107

Neat Bobbins

Keep your bobbin storage neat and tangle-free by winding the thread tail around the bottom of the bobbin and pulling it tight.

Tape to the Rescue

Rescue Tape is a wonderful way to keep your belt in place. A small patch of this two-sided tape will keep straps and belts from slipping—for hours! Be sure to remove it before laundering. It will stick to other fabrics and leave a dark, sticky stain. Ask for it at your local fabric stores.

Try using double-sided Scotch Tape to keep coverings in place. It conquers those stray hairs as well as keeping on little girls' coverings where a pin won't hold.

Notes

BITS & PIECES

BITS & PIECES

110

Notes

Resources

CLOTILDE INC. 4301 N Federal Hwy. 200 • Fort Lauderdale, FL 33308-5209
A great mail order resource for home sewing supplies.

FRIENDS PATTERNS .... 1006 Elm St. • Rolfe, IA 50581
Offering patterns for modest clothing for men, women, boys, and girls.
For a catalog, send $1.00.

THE HIDING PLACE .... P.O. Box 1946 • Vashon, WA 98070-1946
Offering patterns for coverings.

HOME-SEW .... P.O. Box 4099 • Bethlehem, PA 18018-0099

YODER BARGAIN STORE
Ask for catalog.   7806 Salt Creek Rd. • Fredericksburg, OH 44627

Notes

Notes

Notes

114

Index

Sewing Machine

Laundry & Pressing

Bits & Pieces

INDEX

118